INTRODUCTION

In 1926, a princess was born in Mayfair, London. Named Elizabeth after her mother, she was also known as "Lilibet" in tribute to her initial attempts to pronounce her own name as a child. She was third in line to the throne, behind her uncle and her father. However, Queen Elizabeth II ascended the throne in 1952 when she was 25 years old, after her uncle abdicated in 1936 and her father passed away in 1952. Her coronation was held on June 2, 1953, at Westminster Abbey, and she rose to the occasion, celebrating jubilee after jubilee and managing the expectations of her and her family. Her reign lasted 70 years and 214 days, making it the longest of any British monarch, let alone the longest of any female monarch, in history.

One of the most influential icons of the 20th and 21st centuries, Queen Elizabeth II was known for her poise, patience, and peacefulness. This coloring book is a unique tribute to her life and rule, featuring 32 line art designs of regal portraits, historical moments, public appearances, royal properties, commemorative mailing stamps, and even her beloved four-legged friends. Along with its original full-color photograph, each illustration is also complemented with insightful captions to read about her legacy as queen and even some fun, personal facts about her and her favorite things.

Queen Elizabeth II's reign was the longest of any British monarch in history, let alone a female monarch, that lasted from 1952 until her passing in 2022.

The Early Years

Queen Elizabeth II was born to parents King George VI and Queen Elizabeth Bowes-Lyon (then Duke and Duchess of York) on April 21, 1926, at 2:40 am. Had she been born five days later on April 26, she would have shared her birthday with her parents' third wedding anniversary! From 1927 until 1936, little Princess Elizabeth lived with her parents and her younger sister, Princess Margaret Rose (born on August 21, 1930), at their favorite royal property, 145 Piccadilly. A beautiful

April 21, 1926:
Princess Elizabeth II is born.

January 20, 1936:
Princess Elizabeth's grandfather, King George V, passes away. Her uncle, Edward VIII, ascends the throne.

December 10, 1936:
Edward VIII abdicates the throne and Elizabeth's father, George VI, becomes king.

October 13, 1940:
Princess Elizabeth makes her first radio speech to the public at age 14.

home with a stone façade, the family of four were very fond of the home and the memories made there with their beloved nannies, governesses, dogs, and even a pet parrot named Jimmie!

On January 20, 1936, Princess Elizabeth's grandfather, King George V, passed away. Her uncle, Edward VIII, was the next heir to the throne, her father was second in line, and she was third. But in a surprising and dramatic turn of events, her uncle abdicated the throne on December 10, 1936, not even one full year since his ascension. This monumental shift changed everything for George VI and his daughter, and he swiftly began to introduce his heir to the daily processes of ruling. She was a dutiful student and took all the changes of her day-to-day life in stride, even that of moving out of their beloved 145 Piccadilly property and into Buckingham Palace. And while George VI and his wife Elizabeth never really wanted to rule, they were determined to do it as best as they could.

While she was Princess at the time of her service, Queen Elizabeth was the first female within a royal family to have served in the military.

April 21, 1942:
The princess is appointed as a colonel of the Grenadier Guards.

May 8, 1945:
World War II ends and Princess Elizabeth anonymously celebrates VE Day with the public.

July 9, 1947:
Prince Philip and Princess Elizabeth publicly announce their engagement.

November 20, 1947:
The royal wedding between Prince Philip (26) and Princess Elizabeth (21) takes place.

A Queen in the Making

When Princess Elizabeth was 14 years old, she made her first radio speech to the public on the Children's Hour broadcast on October 13, 1940. A voice for the children among the fear and uncertainty that World War II was bringing, it was a comforting broadcast that the country needed, especially coming from a child. But even during such a turbulent time, (Buckingham Palace was attacked 16 times and suffered nine direct hits!), she continued her studies and poised herself as a true heir and queen-in-training. She began helping the Dig for Victory campaign, her father would relay information to her from the official Red Boxes, and she took on several public roles, including the Presidency of the RSPCC and Queen Elizabeth Hospital for Children.

By the time she was 16, she was officially appointed as a colonel of the Grenadier Guards and her first official public engagement was her inspection of the troops in Windsor's forecourt on April 21, 1942. After that, Elizabeth was eager to take on any opportunity that came her way, from becoming a Sea Ranger and accompanying her parents on official visits to exploring shipyards, inspecting squadrons, being appointed as one of the five counsellors of state, and more. Eventually the Auxiliary Territorial Service (ATS) was established in 1938 as a female branch of the army, and Elizabeth was appointed as an honorary second subaltern in February 1945. Within a few months, she was an honorary junior commander.

On May 8, 1945, crowds gathered to celebrate VE Day at Piccadilly Circus, and King George VI even granted his daughters permission to celebrate and mingle with the crowds where Elizabeth and Margaret spent a few anonymous hours dancing in the streets.

A Family of Her Own

The young romance between Elizabeth and Philip was endearing to the public, especially at a time when monarchs usually married for duty and not for love. Their wedding was arguably the most celebrated event of the 20th century, coming at a time when the public was weary from war.

Prince Philip, Duke of Edinburgh, was born on June 10, 1921, on the Greek island of Corfu and was the only son of Prince Andrew of Greece and Denmark and Princess Alice of Battenberg. He wasn't a British subject at birth, but did have family ties to England. His early life was plagued by war, neglect, tragedy, and endurance, and his family never truly settled down. By the time Philip was 10 years old, his mother was admitted to a Swiss sanatorium, his father had fled to France with a mistress, and his sisters all married and moved away to Germany. Luckily, Philip's maternal grandmother, Princess Victoria, sent him to live with his uncle George, who would be Philip's guardian for the next seven years.

Princess Elizabeth was only eight when she first met her third cousin Philip at a wedding, and then again when she was 13 and he was 18 at the Royal Navy College in Dartmouth. After this visit, they would exchange letters and Elizabeth would keep a photo of him by her bed. However, World War II had begun and the couple would be separated for six years while Philip served in the British Royal Navy and the princess trained as a driver and mechanic for the ATS.

When the war was over in 1945, the pair was still in love and Elizabeth's father invited Philip to Balmoral in 1946. It was during this visit he asked the king for permission to marry the princess and he consented with the condition it remains a secret until Elizabeth

November 14, 1948:
The couple welcomes the birth of their first child, Prince Charles.

August 15, 1950:
Princess Elizabeth welcomes their second child, Princess Anne.

February 6, 1952:
At age 25, Princess Elizabeth receives the news her father, King George VI, has passed away, making her queen.

June 2, 1953:
The coronation of Queen Elizabeth II takes place at Westminster Abbey in London.

In post-WWII times, rationing was in effect for the people of the UK, even the royal family. While many women sent Princess Elizabeth their clothing coupons, Elizabeth mailed them all back and had to save up her own coupons in order to pay for her wedding dress.

turned 21 in April 1947. Her family was a bit reluctant and questioned whether Philip was a suitable choice for Elizabeth for various reasons, including the fact that even though he was a prince, he was left penniless from the tumult of his own family. Of course, they eventually accepted their daughter's relationship

and the engagement was made public on July 9, 1947. On November 20, 1947, the pair was wed and they were soon off on their honeymoon to Broadlands in Hampshire and then to Birkhall Lodge.

And just 12 months later, on November 14, 1948, a prince named Charles was born to the happy couple.

November 1953–May 1954:
Queen Elizabeth and Prince Philip embark on the longest ever Commonwealth tour.

February 19, 1960:
A second son is born to the queen, Prince Andrew.

March 10, 1964:
Elizabeth gives birth to her youngest son and last child, Prince Edward.

July 29, 1981:
Prince Charles marries Lady Diana Spencer.

The public was so overjoyed about the birth that they were celebrating outside the palace singing and partying into the early morning hours and were asked to keep their celebrations quieter to let Elizabeth and her baby rest! Bonfires around the country were also lit, which had been a tradition for centuries every time a new monarch arrived into the world. Unfortunately, this was also around the same time King George VI's health began to decline. Princess Elizabeth continued to take on more responsibilities, and then, on August 15, 1950, Elizabeth gave birth to a baby girl, Princess Anne.

As queen-in-waiting, Elizabeth and Philip had to go on many visits around the globe (they even lived in Malta for some time), and it was while they were in Kenya on February 6, 1952, that she received the news her father had passed away in his sleep at the age of 56. Princess Elizabeth was now Queen Elizabeth.

Her Reign

She was 25 years old when she became the new queen of the United Kingdom. Her father was admired by the public and he was a firm ally with Winston Churchill, who gave an emotional eulogy and has gone down in history as one of his most eloquent speeches. Churchill went on to be a mentor for his friend's daughter and now queen until his retirement in 1955.

Queen Elizabeth II's coronation took almost 18 months to plan! On June 2, 1953, over 27 million people watched the coronation ceremony in the UK, and an estimated 277 million were watching worldwide. Between November 1953 and May 1954, the Queen and Prince Philip would travel to Bermuda, Jamaica, Fiji, Tonga, New Zealand, Australia, the Cocos Islands, Ceylon, Aden, Uganda, Malta, and Gibraltar for the Commonwealth Tour. Known for being one of the most ambitious journeys ever taken by the British monarchy, this world-circling tour made a profound impression on the Queen and her subjects.

While Queen Elizabeth would be greeted by cheering crowds in different countries of the Commonwealth, more countries were gaining independence throughout the 1950s, including Sudan, Malaya, and Ghana. Within a decade, nearly all of the remaining colonies in Africa became independent of Britain, as well as the Caribbean, Jamaica, Trinidad, Tobago, Barbados, and Honduras. In the decades that followed, more countries would break away and Queen Elizabeth would continue her travels to meet with the heads of government, as she remained interested in the overall welfare of the independent countries across the Commonwealth.

In 1960, Queen Elizabeth gave birth to another son, Prince Andrew, and then finally Prince Edward in 1964 when she was just one month shy of her 38th birthday. By that time, she had been on the throne for over a decade and was more confident in her challenging responsibilities of being both a queen and a mother. However, there were still hurdles. She received an assassination threat, booing, and a riot during a 10-day tour through Canada. The royal household was also shaken by the discovery of an internal Soviet spy on staff as a Surveyor of the Queen's Pictures.

While the 60s and 70s were a time of monumental cultural change, the 80s proved to be both triumphant and turbulent with many highs and lows. Prince Charles announced his engagement to Lady Diana Spencer in February 1981, and they were married on July 29, 1981. This event marked a shift in public and media focus to

October 14, 1981:
During a visit to New Zealand, a teenager makes a failed assassination attempt on the queen. Just four months before, another attempt was made by a teenager during the annual Trooping the Colour ceremony.

July 9, 1982:
A man broke into Queen Elizabeth's bedroom while she was sleeping, but she awoke and was able to call for help.

October 15, 1986:
Queen Elizabeth becomes the first (and only) British monarch to visit Chinese mainland.

February 6, 1992:
A more low-key event, Queen Elizabeth's Ruby Jubilee celebrates the 40th anniversary of her ascension.

the younger monarchs, especially when William and Harry were born in 1982 and 1984. The Queen's role was focused on state and constitutional matters, while Diana rose to fame.

While they didn't always agree and see eye-to-eye, Queen Elizabeth II and Prime Minister Margaret Thatcher worked together respectfully and became friends. Foreign politics dominated the 1980s, and the Queen traveled extensively to support ties between Britain and various countries around the world. She made 17 state visits, with five taking place in 1980 alone. Among her trips was a groundbreaking stay in China in 1986 in an effort to improve their relations, and this would be one of the most iconic moments of her reign. By 1990, she was known as one of the most experienced and traveled heads of state in the world. She was also invited to the newly unified Germany within months of the fall of the Berlin Wall.

With all her accomplishments, including credit and praise for her behind-the-scenes role in ending apartheid in South Africa, there were many assassination attempts made on her. She even awoke one night to find a man in her bedroom, but instead of pressing charges, she made sure he received psychiatric support.

More royals were married, and their family was expanding with the birth of more grandchildren to the Queen and she happily took on the role of a doting grandmother. Five of her eight grandchildren were born in the 1980s. But with a growing family of the next generation of royals and an ever-changing world came more media attention. Reports did begin to swirl of marital difficulties, and especially that between Charles and Diana. But while the young royals were landing on the front pages of news articles and magazines, the Queen was dealing with political upheaval from Margaret Thatcher's fall from power, the Gulf War, and her triumphant address to the US Congress—a first for a British monarch.

The 1990s was known as Elizabeth's annus horribilis, especially the year of 1992 where separations, divorces, fires, scandalous photos, tell-all books, and more dominated the news. Charles and Diana announced their separation in March, and Princess Anne and her husband officially divorced in April. A warts-and-all book was published in June revealing the personal struggles of Princess Diana, Prince Charles, and his alleged affair. Unflattering photographs were published of Sarah Ferguson, the Duchess of York (and Prince Andrew's ex-wife), in August. A massive fire that took 15 hours to put out destroyed over 100 rooms and 7,000 square feet of Windsor Castle in November. On top of it all, the public was informed they would have to foot the bill for repairs, at a time during a recession and when the Queen paid no taxes on her private income. However, the Queen made tax contributions and even covered 70% of the costs herself. Nevertheless, it was a somber year and more strife would follow.

The Monarchy in the 21st Century

Queen Elizabeth's Diamond Jubilee celebrations took place in the summer of 2012, marking her 60-year reign. This celebration also signified the next generation of royals, including the Queen's heirs. She supported a slimmed-down structure of the monarchy and ways to make the royal family relevant to the modernized country it served. Prince William and Prince Harry

November 20, 1992:
A fire breaks out in Windsor Castle, destroying over 100 rooms.

August 31, 1997:
Princess Diana tragically dies in a car accident in Paris, France.

April 9, 2005:
Prince Charles remarries to Camilla Parker Bowles.

September 9, 2015:
The queen officially becomes the longest-serving monarch in UK history.

began to promote their own causes and would carry out royal engagements, projects, and appearances more widely across the country. By the end of the 2010s, Elizabeth II put her energy into ensuring her heir, Prince Charles, would inherit a treasured role. By this time, William and Harry had wed and started families of their own. She scaled back her overseas travel while Prince Charles increased his own, including groundbreaking trips to the Republic of Ireland and Cuba.

In June 2022, Queen Elizabeth II hit another major milestone: her Platinum Jubilee. A celebration of her 70th anniversary of her ascension was historic. At the time of her passing on September 8, 2022, her reign had lasted 70 years and 214 days, making it the longest of any British monarch, let alone the longest of any female monarch, in history.

At her request, Queen Elizabeth II's coronation ceremony was the first one ever to be broadcast on radio and television around the world. Over 277 million people tuned in!

February 6, 2017:
The queen's Sapphire Jubilee takes place to celebrate 65 years since her ascension.

November 20, 2017:
Queen Elizabeth and Prince Philip celebrate the 70th wedding anniversary,

April 9, 2021:
Just two months short of his 100th birthday, Prince Philip dies.

September 8, 2022:
Queen Elizabeth II passes away at age 96.

COLOR BY MALIA HERRON (MARKERS)

COLOR BY MALIA HERRON (MARKERS)

COLOR BY MALIA HERRON (MARKERS)

COLOR BY MALIA HERRON (MARKERS)

Design Originals, www.D-Originals.com

COLOR BY MALIA HERRON (MARKERS)

Queen Elizabeth and Prince Philip attend The Trooping of the Colour in Buckingham Palace in June 2017, which can be described as the monarch's "second birthday" that celebrates her ascension! The historic ceremony includes parading soldiers, horses, musicians, and more in a stunning display of fanfare and military precision.

Queen Elizabeth was only eight when she met her future husband, and then again when she was 13 and he was 18. They were eventually married on November 20, 1947, when she was 21 years old.

When she was 25 years old, Princess Elizabeth became Queen. Her coronation took nearly 18 months to plan and an estimated 277 million people watched the ceremony worldwide!

W hile the royals greet many fans and make time for walkabouts
through adoring crowds, they are not allowed to sign autographs.
This is to prevent anyone from forging their signature!

Madame Tussauds Wax Museum is a major tourist attraction in London, England and has had a close relationship with the British Royal Family since they first opened in 1884. As a part of their Royal Dress Collection that displays several historic gowns worn by Her Majesty, they also created a stunning replica of the Imperial State Crown that was showcased from 1956 until the early 1970s.

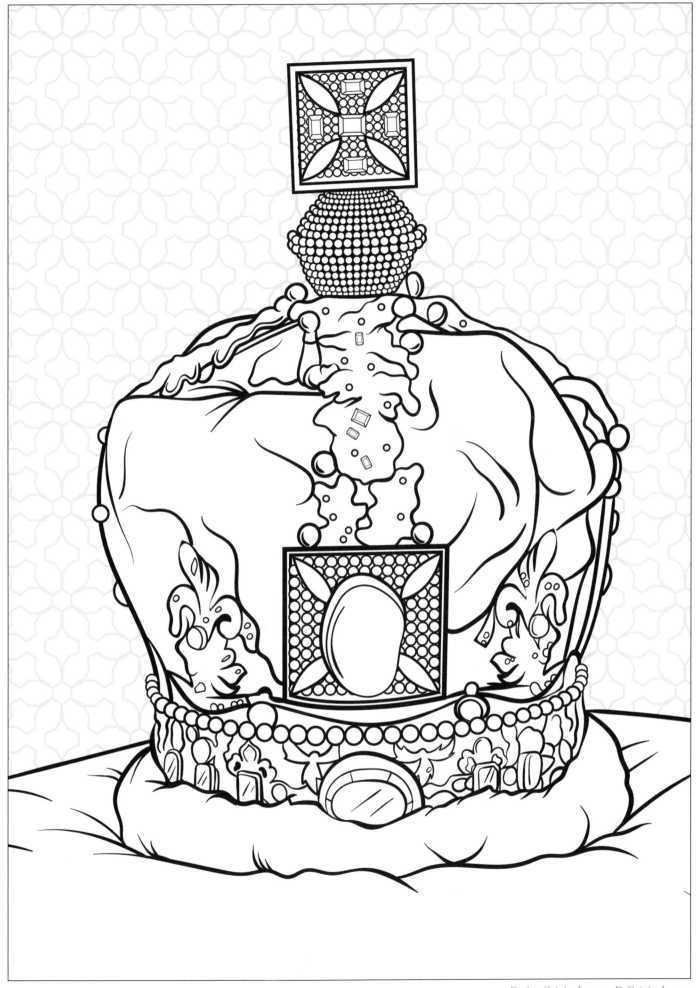

Madame Tussauds has created over 20 life-like wax figures of Queen Elizabeth II at various stages of her life, the first being created in 1928 when she was just two years old! In collaboration with Buckingham Palace, this 23rd figure of Queen Elizabeth II features her white and silver lace dress she wore at her official Diamond Jubilee and is covered in 53,000 Swarovski crystals.

If you ever wondered why Queen Elizabeth would always wear bright colors for her appearances, it was for a good reason. She favored stand-out colors so that the crowds could easily see her!

The Royal Coat of Arms is just one of many beautiful details on and around the iron gates of Buckingham Palace. Another intricate emblem includes a lion to symbolize England and a unicorn to symbolize Scotland. There are also tributes to past monarchs, as well as sculptures that represent Australia, Canada, and South and West Africa.

The official title of a Beefeater is 'The Yeomen Warders of Her Majesty's Royal Palace and Fortress the Tower of London, and Members of the Sovereign's Body Guard of the Yeoman Guard Extraordinary.' But because that's such a mouthful, they're more widely known as Beefeaters, even though it isn't entirely clear where that name came from. The most likely explanation is they used to be told to eat as much meat as they pleased when they were invited to dine with the King.

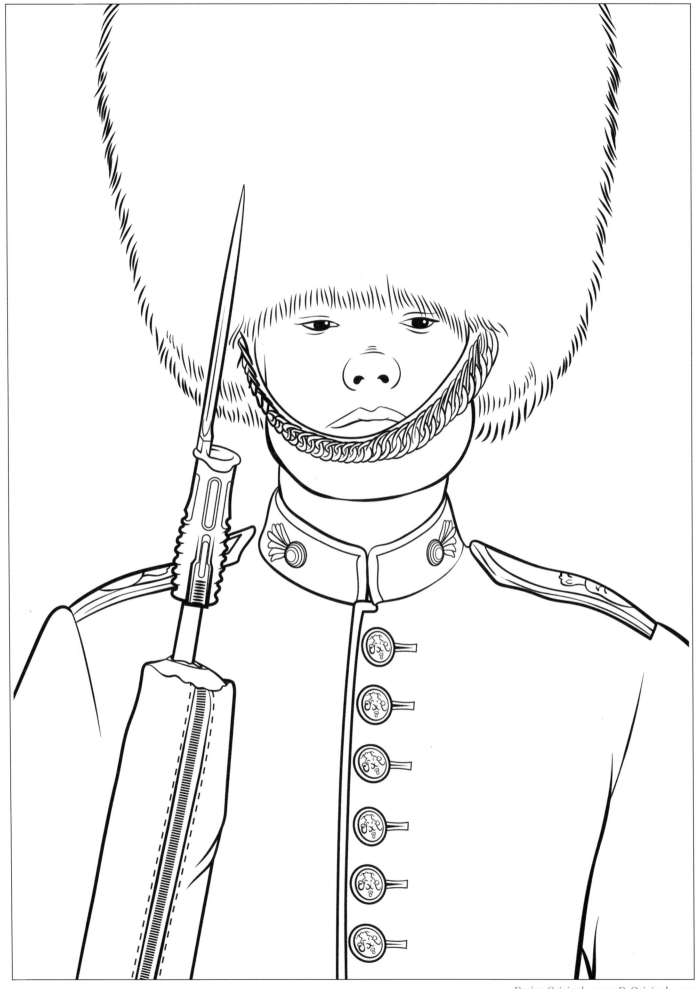

Queen Elizabeth II was known to have a delightful sense of humor and it is said she could make a room burst into laughter for her impression of a Concorde landing.

When the Auxiliary Territorial Service was established in 1938 as a female branch of the army, Elizabeth was appointed as an honorary second subaltern in February 1945. Within a few months, she was an honorary junior commander.

Among many accomplishments, Queen Elizabeth was known for her poise, patience, and peacefulness. As one of the most experienced and traveled heads of state in the world, she made many groundbreaking trips around the world to smooth relations and ease tension.

Y ou may think a purse is just a purse, but the Queen would actually send secret messages to her staff using her handbag! For example, if she was attending a dinner and placed her bag on the table, that would let her staff know she was ready to leave soon. If she placed it on the floor, that meant she needed help getting out of the conversation she was having.

On Christmas morning, it is tradition for the royal family to greet the public outside the Church of St. Mary Magdelene. Many royals have been baptized at this historic church, including Princess Diana!

The year 2012 marked the 60th anniversary of Queen Elizabeth's accession, which is historically known as the Diamond Jubilee of Elizabeth II. While the Queen and the Duke of Edinburgh toured the United Kingdom, other members of the royal family toured the rest of the Commonwealth as the monarch's representatives.

Here, Queen Elizabeth II is seated in the Royal Coach at the Queen's Birthday Parade on June 15, 2013 in London, UK. The Queen's Birthday Parade takes place every June and is known as the Trooping of the Colour to celebrate her ascension, or "second" birthday.

With over a million visitors each year, the Windsor Castle is a fascinating landmark! Originally built in the 11th century, it contains a 2.65-mile driveway, an impressive art collection, 300 fireplaces, the oldest working kitchen in the country, and nearly 400 clocks. One person is responsible for the upkeep of the clocks, and it takes him 16 hours to wind them forward in the spring and 11 to 23 hours to wind them backward!

Did you know Queen Elizabeth II was the first female within a royal family to have served in the military?

Did you know Queen Elizabeth II's portraits graced more than 100 currencies and banknotes from over 20 countries and territories? This whopping number of appearances from more countries than any other person in history landed her a Guinness World Record!

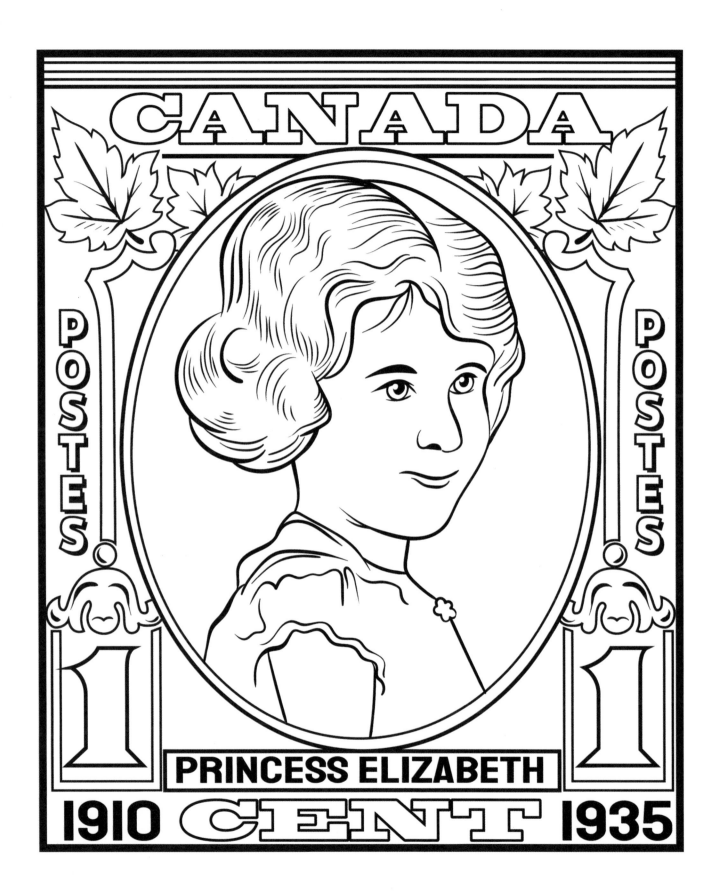

While little is known about the interior of the Balmoral Castle, its exterior was built entirely from local granite from the estate's own land. Its Scottish baronial architecture, a style of the 19th century Gothic revival, gives a nod to the tower houses from the Middle Ages.

From 1949 to 1951, Queen Elizabeth II, a Princess and a newlywed at the time, lived in Malta with her new groom, Philip, while he was serving aboard the HMS Magpie. It was one of the few opportunities they had to enjoy a normal life. Her father George VI passed away in 1952 and she was crowned Queen soon after.

It was widely known that the Queen loved corgis, so much so that she owned over 30 of them throughout her lifetime! A corgi of her own named Susan was gifted to her on her 18th birthday, and many of her corgis since then descended directly from Susan!

Queen Elizabeth II was very well-spoken. In fact, she was fluent in at least six languages and could both read and write in English, French, Greek, Italian, Spanish, and Latin!

Since her passing, many Madame Tussauds Wax Museum locations around the globe have placed condolence books next to her figure for guests to leave a special tribute to the queen.

Did you know that the Queen also invented a breed of dog? Her corgi once had a puppy with a dachshund, and a new species of dog was born called dorgis!

At the conclusion of each Trooping the Colour ceremony, the royal family stands on the balcony at Buckingham Palace to watch a fly-past of the Royal Air Force.

Queen Elizabeth II gave many speeches during her 70-year reign, but among her most memorable was her first-ever public speech on the radio at age 14 where she addressed and comforted her peers affected by World War II. She'd continue to deliver speeches until she was 96 years old, just months before her death.

K nown for wearing bright colors, she was especially fond of wearing the color blue. But blue also had some hidden meanings! Associated with many things, ranging from art and business to the military and monarchy, she also wore blue to represent her allegiance to Scotland, as the country held a very special place in her heart.

There are 29 billion coins currently in circulation featuring Queen Elizabeth II's portrait in the United Kingdom, as well as Australia, New Zealand, and Canada.

Did you know Queen Elizabeth II is the most pictured person on stamps in history worldwide? While it's quite an impressive feat, that also makes it hard to know exactly how many there have been since 1952! Known as the Machin portrait, it's estimated that stamp alone was printed more than 220 billion times in various colors and denominations!

AUSTRALIA

50c

Coronation 1953

2003

The Elizabeth Tower, which is more commonly known as Big Ben, is one of London's most infamous landmarks. Technically, Big Ben is the name of the bell inside the clock tower. It rang for the first time on May 31, 1859.

There are over 25 Madame Tussauds Wax Museum locations worldwide! In 2019, Queen Elizabeth was on display in Bangkok, Thailand. During her reign, she visited Thailand twice and was very fond of the country and its royal family.